Dad's
white-water ride

We are going out of
town today. Dad has
packed swimming bags
and a picnic. Dad's boat
is on the car roof.

He's taking us to the river!
Dad says he found a good
spot when he was looking
for deer once.

Here we are at the swimming spot. There is a wide gravel strip by the still water.

We go with Dad up the steep track. He says the river has a sheer drop. Then there is a foaming white-water run.

We stop where we can see
the sheer drop in the river.
"Wait here," says Dad.
He keeps going. We wait.

We peer through the bushes. Can that be Dad, there on the river? He's a mere dot, far away. The water is fast. Dad is too.

Dad gets to the sheer
drop. Over he goes! He
vanishes, then bobs up
in the foaming water. We
cheer as loudly as we can.

He steers the boat down the white water. He tries to veer away from rocks as he careers along.

And now he is in still water. We run down the track. We get to where he is steering the boat to the river side. We try to pull the boat in.

"I'll get out, then you have a go in the boat," he says.

"But only in still water," he adds. He sounds quite severe but he is smiling.

Dad looks at us and cheers.
We have loads of fun and we
adhere to the still-water rule!

Words to blend

deer	sheer	peer
cheer	careers	steering
here	mere	severe
adhere	veer	cheers
steers	gravel	picnic
foaming	loudly	quite

Before reading

Synopsis: The children and Dad go to the river. The kids watch as Dad takes his boat out into the foaming white-water run. What an adventure!

Review phonemes and graphemes: /oo/ (moon) ui, ou; /oo/ (yoo) ew, ue, u-e, u; /oo/ (look) u, oul; /or/ aw, al, au, oor, our, ore; /ur/ ir, or, ear, er; /ow/ ou; /oi/ oy

Focus phoneme: /ear/   **Focus graphemes:** ere, eer

Story discussion: Look at the cover, and read the title together. Ask: *What can you see on the cover? Have you ever gone in a boat like Dad's? What kind of book do you think this is – fiction or non-fiction? How do you know?*

Link to prior learning: Remind children that the sound /ear/ as in 'hear' can also be spelled 'eer' and 'ere'. Turn to page 8 and ask children to find a word with each spelling of the /ear/ sound (sheer, here).

Vocabulary check: sheer: very steep – 'a sheer drop' means 'a very steep drop'.

Decoding practice: Display the words 'careers', 'here', 'veer' and 'severe'. Can children circle the letter string that makes the /ear/ sound, and read each word?

Tricky word practice: Display the word 'once'. Remind children that there are two tricky parts in this word: 'o', which makes the sound /wu/, and 'ce', which makes the sound /s/. Practise reading and spelling this word.

After reading

Apply learning: Discuss the book. Ask: *Do you think Dad's ride looked fun? Would you want to try, or would you prefer to stay in still water?*

Comprehension

- When did Dad find a good spot at the river? (when he was looking for deer)
- Does Dad go over the sheer drop? (yes)
- Are the children allowed to have a go in the boat? (yes, but only in still water)

Fluency

- Pick a page that most of the group read quite easily. Ask them to reread it with pace and expression. Model how to do this if necessary.
- Challenge children to read page 10 to show that what was happening was exciting. Remind them to pay attention to punctuation like exclamation marks.
- Practise reading the words on page 17.

Tricky words review

of	the	once
says	was	are
there	where	water
have	who	today
whole	friend	through